Declare Yourself WEALTHY

By Sonya L Thompson

www.oilandtheglory.com

Dedication

I dedicate this book to my grandmother Cora Lee Neal, who has gone on to be with the Lord. She was my inspiration. My grandmother was a strong unrelenting woman of God who stayed on her knees and touched heaven on my behalf. It's because of her prayers and declarations of faith that I am who I am today. No matter what I embarked upon she always encouraged me. If she were here today I know she would be proud of me.

She passed the baton of faith into my hands as she finished her race, and I will run with the same perseverance and unrelenting commitment she instilled in me, until I see her again. I will always carry the memory of her in my heart and the sound of her sweet voice in my ears telling me "You can do it!"

Table of Contents

Introduction

Wealth means different things to different people. For some people wealth relates only to money. For others, their health, marriage and children represent wealth. In this book **"Declare Yourself Wealthy,"** the goal is to apply the Word of God to all of these areas, and specifically to the area of finances. Make no mistake about it the intended purpose of this book is for you to declare yourself wealthy, rich, and abundant in your finances. Also included are declarations which cover the other areas of your life as well.

It makes no sense to flourish in other areas and walk around living from paycheck to paycheck! This is not your Father's plan for your life. Because of my stormy financial past, I personally take great issue with the spirit of poverty, lack, debt and limitation. No one could convince me that barely getting by was the way God wanted me to live. After all, He is my Father and He loved me enough to send Jesus as a Son who gave up His very life just for me. How could a God like this withhold anything from me? With this in mind, I began a journey to uncover the truth about financial wealth, based on what my Father says is the truth.

Poverty, lack and debt are a spirit and mindset. They have been adopted based upon our upbringing, the reports of society and the conditions we can see. A countless number of people are barely getting by financially in large part due to the words they speak. Based upon what we see, we have passed a verdict of poverty over our lives and will eventually hand this way of living over as an inheritance to our children, who will continue to perpetuate what we term as a "generational curse."

This cycle will never stop until someone stands up and says enough! I hope that someone is you. I pray you are the agent for your family who will stand up and make a decision to trust in the Word of God, and change the verdict over your finances, family, business and employment by **"Declaring Yourself Wealthy!"**

Chapter 1

It's in Your Mouth

If you have read any of my books you will find out one thing I never cease to mention is the power of your words. The moment you grasp the power your Father has given you through your words, is the moment you will be able to take hold of the course of your life and begin to see and experience an almost instant and dramatic change for the better! You will have to embrace a new language, the Word language, to experience the change I am talking about. This simply means you make a conscious decision to speak the Word only, regardless of the situation you are face to face with. Up until now, your words may have possibly been hurting you or others. Your words may have caused you to destroy your health, finances or even abort the opportunities God has sent your way. But now, it's time for a new way to do things.

A little History

To get the full impact of this book, I have to take some time to give you a little background information about who you are and why your words are so very important. Genesis says you & I were made in the image and likeness of the Father. God is a spirit and you are a spirit, who possesses a soul and lives in a body. You have a body because it's the only way for a spirit to legally operate in the earth realm. That's another lesson so take my word for it this time. That's why you are filled with the Holy Spirit so your Father can have access to this earth realm through you. A sprit can only have access in the earth through a flesh and blood body. Because Satan is a copy cat, this is the same way he possesses people to carry out his evil desires on the earth, by gaining access to their body.

God is a spirit with a soul (mind, emotions and will) and He speaks. You are a speaking spirit just like your Heavenly Father. He handed you the power to create, dissemble and rearrange with the words of your mouth. You have the power to make changes in any area of your life which does not line up with His Word.

In the beginning when God created and even when He replenished the earth after the fall of Lucifer, He spoke faith filled words. He said many times in Genesis chapter one, "Let there be." Every time He spoke He saw. Not once did He declare something and nothing happened. God said in **Isaiah 55:11**, His Word would not return void. His words always come back with what He sent them out to retrieve. That's a powerful concept to grasp. Of course we expect God to have these kinds of results! After all, He is God! Words always come back with what they have been sent out to retrieve, when they are sent out with faith (a full persuasion of something's occurrence). Since you are created in His image and likeness, this means your words will come back with something good or bad.

Take an honest inventory of your life and remember a time when you spoke a negative report and it showed up just like you said it would. When it showed up, what did you say? "I knew it. I said that was going to happen!" You see it works for you too. Your faith filled words don't come back void either. Someone may say, "Oh, are you trying to say I am God?" No, there is only one God, but I remember reading in my Bible where Jesus said you and I are gods on this earth.

Jesus answered them, "Is it not written in your Law, 'I have said you are gods' If he called them 'gods,' to whom the word of God came—and Scripture cannot be set aside— what about the one whom the Father set apart as his very own and sent into the world? Why then do you accuse me of blasphemy because I said, I am God's Son?"
(John 10:34-36).

Jesus quoted this from Psalm eighty-two verse six. This does not mean you are God but it does mean you and I are mighty ones on this earth whom God has given "godlike" qualities and authority to carry out His Kingdom assignment on this earth. You and I are god-men just like Jesus when He walked the earth. He demonstrated for you, the authority you are supposed to have on the earth. I will give you an analogy which makes this a little clearer before we move on. If I take a dropper of water out of the ocean, this is not the ocean itself, but a part of the ocean. Even though it's a smaller amount, it's still ocean water. It's not the whole but only part. Likewise, you are not God (the ocean), but you are a part (the drop) of Him with the same image and likeness as the whole. You're made in His likeness and image. You can do some powerful things on this earth when you embrace this truth.

Our God is a God who used words to create what He desired, and now you have got the power! God is still speaking, through you. With this knowledge in hand, I think it would be wise from this point on to watch your words. You are creating, disassembling and rearranging every time you open your mouth. Selah (pause and think of that)! The question to consider is this: Am I creating an accurate picture of the image and likeness of my Father?

Chapter 2

Read Your Nametag

Have you ever attended a large function where you were assigned a name tag? What's the purpose of this? So you can be identified correctly. My name is Sonya. So, if I were wearing a name tag which plainly identified my name as Sonya and someone came up and called me Sophia, this has happened, I wouldn't like this at all. I would quickly tell them my name is Sonya and of course the person would apologize and call me by the correct name.

I shared the example above for a very valid reason. What does your name tag read today? If I were to ask you the name of your finances what would your nametag read? Does it read: Lack, Broke, Not Enough, Just Enough, Fixed Income, Minimum Wage, or Insufficiency? If I were to ask you to do the same for your physical body what would it read? Would it read: Overweight, Cancer, High blood Pressure, Diabetes, Depression, Mental Illness, or ADHD? My friend listen to me, you can't get mad at God and life because you are being singled out by the nametag you have assigned to yourself! The situations in your life have not just shown up out of nowhere. They are what they are because you have signed the nametag with your words.

My heart is stirred by a noble theme as I recite my verses for the king; <u>my tongue</u> is the pen of a skillful writer (Psalm 45:1).

It looks like the pen is in your mouth! You are the one who recited the name of your finances before the king. God didn't do it. God has not allowed it. You've made the decree over your finances as "not enough." You've made the decree over your marriage, body, children and so forth. So the Law of life & death hears the voice of your words and makes sure your circumstances agree with your nametag.

You can't expect to be called by a name you haven't put on your nametag. This is like somebody calling me Sophia instead of Sonya. It's not the truth. When they see my name tag clearly, they will correct it. Likewise, the laws of life and death see your name tag because of the words you have spoken. You have received exactly who you say you are, what you say can do, and have every single time! You will not get an apology from the Law of life and death, blessing and cursing which was put in motion in ***Deuteronomy 30:19***. It's time to start using your tongue like the pen of a skilful writer. Wow! That is a mouthful and I pray right now as you read these words the revelation and illumination of the Holy Spirit will enlighten the eyes of your understanding.

Here are some statements I want to leave with you:

- **Your words define you** - You are what you say you are. Whether you like it or not.
- **Your words single you out** – Your words will come back with what you sent them out to retrieve. They are like guided missiles. They will bring just what you ordered.
- **What you say is what you get** – The name you assign on your tag is exactly what your finances, body, marriage and children will be called by the Law of life or the law of death.

Chapter 3

You Need a New Name!

Well, if you have made it this far, I have to say you are serious about making a change in your finances in particular, as well as your health, marriage and any other area which does not line up with or look like what the Word of God says it's supposed to look like.

When I was growing up a person's name meant something. Today people name their children anything which sounds phonetically challenged or stylish! They do this because they don't have a clear understanding of the power of the spoken name. The name you have been assigned means something. Your name is a direct reflection of your nature and your character. To substantiate this, when Adam named the animals, God brought them to him in their living form, but they were not yet alive. He allowed Adam to use the power of his words to impart the nature and character into the animals by naming them. God allowed Adam to do just what He had been doing from the beginning, as we know it.

Now the Lord God had formed out of the ground all the wild animals and all the birds in the sky. He brought them to the man to see what he would name them; and whatever the man called each living creature, that was its name. So the man gave names to all the livestock, the birds in the sky and all the wild animals (Genesis 2:19-20).

The word "name" used here in the Hebrew means "**A mark, a memorial of individuality, authority, or character.**" Whatever Adam called the animals caused them to come to life and take on the individuality, authority, character and nature of their name! Whatever he called them is what they became. From his imagination he spoke life into thus they took on the nature of the name they were assigned.

This process did not stop in the Garden of Eden. Oh no! It continues on today. You are the agent whom God has been entrusted with this ability to create, rearrange, and dismantle the situations in your life and in this earth, through words. I will say it again, you have got the power. Why don't you say it for yourself; "I have got the power!"

So, do you see why you need a new name? It starts and finishes with the words you speak. Your words are your beginning and they are your end. Until you begin the process of assigning a new name to your finances they will never change.

The name tag you have assigned up to this point is exactly why your money situation looks and acts like it does today. Your money looks like lack, broke, not enough and just enough, because you assigned those characteristics to it. The name you have assigned is operating in its authority and power; but we are going to see to it before you finish this book you get a new name in your finances and some other areas too.

Chapter 4

Get Out of Your Senses

The only way to secure a new name for your current financial situation is to first ignore the facts. I focus a lot on the financial realm but you can use this truth in any area of your life. It will work if you work it. This is by far one of the toughest things you're going to have to do. In a nutshell, don't let your words agree with the appearance of your current financial circumstances. Even though adverse circumstances are staring you square in your face, you must refuse to allow your words, which you now realize have great power, to come into agreement with what you can *see, touch, hear, feel, taste or smell*. You are going to have to get out of your **"SENSES."** This means you can't let the facts of what you perceive to be true, to be your ultimate truth. Romans 3:4 says **"Let God be true and every man a liar."** This might sound a bit confusing right now, but allow me the opportunity to make it a little clearer.

I am going to share a very personal account of my own to validate this and then qualify it with Scripture. Though this relates to a recent health issue, the principle can apply to your money and anything else you may be confronted with. A few months ago, I was told I had to have a total hysterectomy because I had an "issue of blood," which had me in an anemic state for quite a few years. I had a surgical procedure a few months prior which seemed to help, but the same cycle of events started all over again. The doctor did some tests, found a very large tumor and told me I had to have a complete hysterectomy. The tests were in and the verdict had been declared. I made error of coming into agreement with it because I just wanted it fixed; therefore I began to make plans for surgery.

A few days or so later, I was sitting at my desk in my office and began to remind myself of the truth of God's Word. I saw myself like the prodigal son and I came to myself. I got out of my senses and remembered **"By His stripes You WERE healed."** I jumped up from my desk and boldly declared, "I will not have this surgery." I commanded my body to "come into alignment with the Word of God, right now! By His Stripes I have already been healed, therefore I walk in my healing right now!" The next thing I did was text my husband and told him not to worry about trying to get time off work because I wasn't going to "take the surgery." I know I should have said I am not going to have the surgery, but for some reason every person I messaged that day, I said, "I am not going to take the surgery." I sent this same message to my Pastor and my First Lady and then I called my mother and told her the same thing. Up until this time I kept complaining about my situation, declaring it over and over but THEN **I decided** I will not take the verdict which had been delivered. I decided I would get out of my senses and speak the truth of the Word of God.

When I made the declaration above, I dispatched my words with the Word of God and everything changed at that moment. Now, here's the thing, in the natural it looked just like it did a few minutes before I jumped up and made the declaration. Nothing changed in the natural for another two weeks or so, but something had changed for me in the spiritual realm. I declared the Word of God in **FAITH (full persuasion of having received what I spoke at that moment)**, and forgot about what I could **SENSE**. Two weeks or so later my body manifested what I declared. The unseen became seen. I got out of my senses, loaded my word speaking ability with God's Word, and got the expected results. I am totally healed! No surgery required, just like I declared. To God be the glory!

In Job 22:28 it says, *"What you decide on will be done, and light will shine on your ways."*

Proverbs 18:21 says, "The tongue has the power of life and death, and those who love it will eat its fruit."

In John 6:63 Jesus said, "My words are Spirit and they are Life."

Just like Job said, I decided I would be healed and it was done. As written in **Proverbs 18:2**, I sent God's Word from my mouth, and now I am eating the fruit of healing. If you want to walk in your healing or stop living from paycheck to paycheck, speak the life giving Word of God into your circumstances and disconnect from your **SENSES**.

You have the power to decide what you will and will not permit to remain in your life! You have the power to overlook those things which appeal to your senses and stick with the truth of God's Word. I have to admit it won't be easy if this isn't the way you're used to doing things, but you have to decide what you really want. It's time for a change! Say what He says over your finances and over your health. Say what He says about your marriage and children and you will eat the fruit of your words. It will be the very verdict you decide!

Chapter 5

Change Your Verdict

When a judge sits at his bench he has the power to enforce a verdict as given by the jury. From this day forward see yourself as the jury of your own life. What do I mean by this? Usually someone from the jury will stand up and read the decree and the judge will lower the gavel to seal the verdict to enforce what has been spoken. You have the power to pronounce the sentence over your life. It's not God's decision, it's yours. The Law of blessing and cursing will respond to the decree you make. Whether you speak the truth of the Word or the lie of this world, you are passing a verdict and will receive the right sentence every time. If you say, "I am broke," then the universal laws are set into motion to ensure the verdict you passed on your life is enforced. You will have what you say, when you speak it with conviction. I will prove this by Scripture of course.

I can't believe the number of Christians who blame God for the negative circumstances which arise in their lives. The usual,

"God is trying to teach me something" line always arises in the midst of difficulty. I beg to differ. If difficulty, struggling and going through seem to mark your path, the first place to check is your mouth. God is not the one responsible! With that being said, I know we live in a fallen world and we are going to encounter some "stuff" in life, BUT all of the things we blame God for are not from God. If it's bad it's not from God. Satan is the one who comes to steal, kill and destroy, as shown in **John 10:10**. Jesus came to give you life and life more abundantly. You have the power to create or change your present circumstances. All you have to do is change your verdict and move forward.

"This day I call the heavens and the earth as witnesses against you that I have set before you life and death, blessings and curses. Now <u>choose </u>life, so that you and your children may live and that you may love the Lord your God, listen to his voice, and hold fast to him. For the Lord is your life, and he will give you many years in the land he swore to give to your fathers, Abraham, Isaac and Jacob"
(Deuteronomy 30:19-20).

Did you notice God put the ball in your court? He gave you the power to choose the verdict. He has set the laws or prosperity in motion for your life, and it's up to you to make a righteous decree which is in line with His Word. If you want what God says you can have, then you must handle your tongue the way you're supposed to.

"You have been trapped by what you said, ensnared by the words of your mouth" (Proverbs 6:2).

The words you speak will either spring you forth to enjoy life or ensnare you in a trap which will lead to death in your finances, marriage and so forth. If you have found yourself in a financial trap and can't seem to get out, it's time to change your verdict.

We have already looked at this verse,

"The tongue has the power of life and death, and those who love it will eat its fruit" (Proverbs 18:21).

It's your tongue and you have power over it. You and I are not controlled by a ventriloquist. Nobody has their hand up your back, speaking for you. There isn't a puppeteer with strings attached to your tongue making you talk contrary to God's Word. You are eating the harvest you planted with your tongue yesterday, today or years ago.

Thou shalt also decree a thing, and it shall be established unto thee: and the light shall shine upon thy ways. (Job 22:28 KJV).

The King James Version uses the word decree. Decree means to declare and to speak; meaning you are the jury who gets to decide your case. Isn't that good news? You thought you were at the mercy of the system. The truth is you have the power. I think it's time to change your verdict don't you? Up to this point you have already proven negative words will get you nowhere. Let's look at how God planned for us to use our word power, in the right way.

Appeal The Verdict

When an unfavorable verdict is passed, the first thing the attorney does is file an appeal. Well, you'll have to do the same thing. You need to appeal the verdict you have spoken over your finances or other areas of your life. Ask God to forgive you and repent of the words you have spoken. Sidebar, repent does not mean crying, falling out or telling God you are a no good low down sinner; it means to think differently after hearing the truth and continue along that course. A repentant heart decides that negative and perverse words spoken over finances or any other area are no longer an option! Now, command crop failure on the negative words you have spoken, go ahead and declare this "I command crop failure on the negative words I have spoken over my finances right now!" Lastly you will now replace your previous verdict by declaring a righteous and just judgment over your finances and life based on what the Word of God says, not based on what you can see.

Chapter 6

Redefine Your Situation

Hidden in this powerful verse of scripture is the only way to redefine your current financial or life situation.

"As it is written, I have made thee a father of many nations, before him whom he believed, even God, who quickeneth the dead, and <u>calleth those things which be not as though they were</u>" (Romans 4:17 KJV).

There it is. This is your golden goose. You have to stop calling it like it is and call it as God says it is. It's just that simple. Your soul (mind emotions and will) can catch up with the truth of God's Word later. You must make the decision to let the truth of God's Word concerning your finances be your **ONLY** truth. Let His word concerning every area of your life be the only truth you will accept and declare. Say this out loud, "I will speak the Word only!" Post this on your refrigerator. Say it to yourself every day. Put it everywhere you will be able to see it to remind yourself of your commitment to redefine your financial situation. So, if you happen to be behind the eight-ball financially and a bill comes in past due, you're not going to go into a tail spin, but you are going to speak the Word only!

What Does Redefining Look Like?

The rest of this book is loaded with powerful declarations for you to retrain your tongue and redefine your finances and anything else you need redefined to line up with the Word of God. I intentionally have the scriptures for meditation labeled as **Scriptures for MEDICATION**. This is not a typo. You are to take the Word of God just like medicine. You need to medicate your soul and heal it of the disease of poverty, lack, and the just enough mentality. See financial lack as a cancer and become aggressive at treating it from this day forward. You are not trying to put it in remission; you must destroy it with the Word of God!

When you begin to do your daily declaration from the back of this book, do them three times per day. Start over at day one when you come to the end of the month. Repetition is the key. Here are examples of what redefining looks like:

Let's say for instance in reality (in the natural sense) you are in a financial bind. No job, no money or not enough money. Whatever the situation, you must declare I am rich! Joel says, **"Let the weak say I am strong,"** why can't you declare riches, health, wisdom, the same way? The key is declaring the opposite of what the situation is by applying the Word like a salve over the wound. Remember, the Word of God is the truth; the situation you face is only a temporary fact.

"Beat your plowshares into swords and your pruning hooks into spears: let the weak say, I am strong" (Joel 3:10 KJV).

If I could put this verse in today's language it would read something like this, "Stop toiling, working two jobs and struggling, and begin to **declare** what you want!" You have worked it your way long enough. You are not under the curse of toiling as in Genesis when Adam fell. No my friend, you are under the blessing of the Lord and you walk in grace and favor.

"But my God shall supply all your need according to his riches in glory by Christ Jesus" (Philippians 4:19 KJV).

In the verse above Paul spoke this in response to the willingness of the Philippians to give to his ministry. If you have a financial seed to plant do it now. If you honestly don't have a dime to your name, tell God you will plant a seed if He will supply it, and then follow through and do it. In the meantime, go ahead and declare, **"My God will supply all my need according to His riches un glory by Christ Jesus!"** Say it with emotion and conviction as you pass this decree over your finances.

You can get far more insight into sowing and reaping in my book, **"Break Out of Poverty Into Financial Abundance."** I would highly recommend adding it to your library. We have received so many testimonies from those whose financial status have increased dramatically from reading this book.

The God you serve and who lives in you is a limitless, infinitely abundant God. Let this image of Him sink into your soul. He is not a just enough God. He is not a God who takes pleasure in seeing you struggle financially. Here is the kicker, He lives IN YOU! Therefore, abundance is already in you. **Psalm 35:27** says He takes pleasure in your prosperity. Your finances have already been redefined by the Word, now it's up to you to come into agreement with what God has already spoken.

Chapter 7

Throw the Book at the Devil

Let me close out the chapters of this book with a very direct warning. Be prepared for an attack of the enemy now that you have decided to stand your ground and change the decree you have made over your finances. Now you may say, "Sonya, this does not sound very exciting to me!" Well, I figured I would warn you in advance. Any time the Word of God goes forth it is Satan's job to come in and steal it before you have a chance to truly plant it in your heart. In Mark chapter four we get a picture of how the enemy is going to attempt to snatch this word from you. I want you to be ready when he comes at you with adverse circumstances. This is merely an attempt to get you to cast away your confidence in the Word. He wants you to open your mouth and declare a negative decree and negate what you have spoken. If you do this, you will be right back where you started from, and I know that's not a good place to be in.

Then Jesus said to them, "Don't you understand this parable? How then will you understand any parable? The farmer sows the word. Some people are like seed along the path, where the word is sown. As soon as they hear it, Satan comes and takes away the word that was sown in them. Others, like seed sown on rocky places, hear the word and at once receive it with joy. But since they have no root, they last only a short time. When trouble or persecution comes because of the word, they quickly fall away. Still others, like seed sown among thorns, hear the word; but the worries of this life, the deceitfulness of wealth and the desires for other things come in and choke the word, making it unfruitful. Others, like seed sown on good soil, hear the word, accept it, and produce a crop—some thirty, some sixty, some a hundred times what was sown" (Mark 4:13-20)

Make it your business to fall in the last category. Hear it, accept it, and manifest the results.

When I was growing up my mom used to say, "The judge threw the book at him." This meant the criminal received the maximum penalty. Here's why I am sharing this with you; it's time for you to throw the book at the devil. When the enemy comes, not **IF** he comes, you have to be prepared to throw the book at him. Jesus showed us in Matthew chapter four exactly what to do when the enemy comes in an attempt to snatch the Word.

Then Jesus was led by the Spirit into the wilderness to be tempted by the devil. After fasting forty days and forty nights, he was hungry. The tempter came to him and said, "If you are the Son of God, tell these stones to become bread." Jesus answered, "*It is written*: 'Man shall not live on bread alone, but on every word that comes from the mouth of God.'" (Matthew 4:1-4)

If you follow this chapter through to verse eleven, you will notice every time the enemy came to get Jesus to declare something other than the Word, He said, **"It is written."**

Jesus made a righteous decree. He declared the Word regardless of what His body felt like or what the enemy showed Him in the natural realm. He kept throwing the book at Satan until he left. You are going to have to do the same. This is how you throw the book (the Word of God) at the devil. Give Him the full force of the Word of God and send Him off someplace else.

Our **"Seeds of Prosperity"** CD is loaded with the prosperous Word of God. Consider adding this to your library to increase your fire power against the enemy. You must have the Word planted in your heart if you are going to throw the book at the devil.

When you make your daily declaration, see yourself being, doing and having exactly what you have declared. See yourself in the jury box passing the right judgment over your finances, over your children, over your body, because you been given the power to **"Declare Yourself Wealthy!"**

God Bless you. I would love to hear from you! Email us your testimonies or connect with us on facebook at:

oilandtheglory

https://www. oilandtheglory.com

info@oilandtheglory.com

Continue to the next section for the daily declarations.

Above the scriptures you will see the heading "*Scriptures for Medication*." This is not a misprint. Take the Word like a medicine and apply it to your life three times per day by decreeing and declaring it with power. I guarantee at the end of thirty-one days your mouth will be "Transformed by the Living Word." Don't put the book away when the month is over. Go back to the beginning and make these decrees and declarations a part of your everyday routine!

Day One

I decree and declare I am a partaker in the abundant Kingdom of the Living God. My Father has a limitless supply of all things in the earth. Everything belongs to Him. There is no shortage or lack of any resources in this earth or in my life. Everything I need, want and desire is available to me right now. As I ask according to the Word, I freely receive. I open my mind today to receive from my Heavenly Father's bounty. I am open and receptive to receive His unlimited, unending supply of all good. I willingly and without reservation receive the inheritance my Father has set aside just for me.

I declare every area of my life flourishes as I yield myself wholly to my Father's desires and plans for my life. I expect and receive an unlimited measure of increase in my finances, relationships, and business affairs today. I am a living epistle read by men. I declare I am the living, breathing, walking and talking manifestation of the blessing of the Lord and I am impacting the lives of others. In Jesus' name!

Scriptures for Medication:

John 3:2 KJV

Beloved, I wish above all things that thou mayest prosper and be in health, even as thy soul prospereth

2 Corinthians 3:3 (AMP)

You show and make obvious that you are a letter from Christ delivered by us, not written with ink but with [the] Spirit of [the] living God, not on tablets of stone but on tablets of human hearts.

Day Two

Thank you Father for the abundance which surrounds me every day! I decree and declare I confidently accept and lay hold of the inheritance you have provided for me. I declare my family lacks nothing because I have tapped into your rich supply. There is no shortage or insufficiency in my life. I serve an all sufficient, abundant and loving Father. Therefore every need has already been supplied.

I declare the desires of my heart are granted to me as they are in line with God's Word. I am thankful for all the Father has provided for me from the foundation of the world. I declare God has done immeasurable more than I can ask, think or imagine. Today, as I permit His mighty power to work in and through me, I am a blessing to all I come in contact with. In Jesus' name!

Scriptures for Medication:

Ephesians 3:20

Now to him who is able to do immeasurably more than all we ask or imagine, according to his power that is at work within us

Philippians 4:19

And my God will meet all your needs according to the riches of his glory in Christ Jesus.

Day Three

I decree and declare this day is crowned with my Father's bounty. I declare, I am an heir and a joint heir with the Lord Jesus Christ. All things which have been given to Him belong to me both in the natural and physical realm. I have life (eternal) and life more abundantly (life here and now) in every area. I am equipped with everything I need and want because I serve a more than enough God. Therefore, my carts overflow with the fatness of my Father's substance.

I declare I am enriched and provided for in every way. My health springs forth speedily. I walk in divine health and healing. My mind is sound; I have the mind of Christ. Today, I make sound and wise decisions for my family, business, employment and finances. I receive all the Father has for me, for He takes pleasure in my prosperity. In Jesus' name!

Scriptures for Medication:

Psalm 65:11-12

You crown the year with your bounty, and your carts overflow with abundance. The grasslands of the wilderness overflow; the hills are clothed with gladness.

1 Corinthians 2:16

"Who has known the mind of the Lord so as to instruct him?" But we have the mind of Christ.

Day Four

Today is the day the Lord has made, fashioned and prepared just for me. Therefore I rejoice and am glad in everything the Father has prepared for me today. I decree and declare no weapon formed against me or my household can prosper because I am the son/daughter of the living God. I declare my health, wealth, and happiness can't be limited, hindered or sabotaged. I walk in the super-abounding grace and favor of the living God today.

I declare I am an ambassador of Christ therefore my provision is richly supplied by the Kingdom of God. I walk in and experience surplus on every side. Christ in me my hope of glory has freed me from all limitations of this world system. I operate on a supernatural level in all areas of my life. I am healthy, wealthy, happy and overtaken by my Father's good pleasure today! I am a blessing to others. In Jesus' name!

Scriptures for Medication:

Isaiah 54:17

No weapon forged against you will prevail, and you will refute every tongue that accuses you. This is the heritage of the servants of the Lord, and this is their vindication from me,"declares the Lord.

Luke 12:32

"Do not be afraid, little flock, for your Father has been pleased to give you the kingdom.

Day Five

I decree and declare I expect my Father's best and highest good to manifest in my life today. I am open and receptive to the avenues by which my increase may come. I declare my increase is not limited or controlled by any earthly system. I will not interrupt the flow of blessing by limiting thoughts or words. My wealth flows to me freely and uninhibited from the north, south east and the west. There is no numbering of the avenues by which my Father will use to bring an abundant harvest into my life today. I declare money comes to me today in increasing amounts from various sources. I draw from my Father's unlimited supply today.

I declare my family is living in the abundant overflow of a limitless, infinite and abundant God. My marriage, children, health, and affairs are overshadowed by the favor of God. I declare He is my Divine source of everything and nothing can stop His good from coming to me. In Jesus' name!

Scriptures for Medication:

Jeremiah32:27

"I am the Lord, the God of all mankind. Is anything too hard for me?

Psalm 91:1-2

Whoever dwells in the shelter of the Most High will rest in the shadow of the Almighty. I will say of the Lord, "He is my refuge and my fortress, my God, in whom I trust."

Day Six

I decree and declare today, I encounter divine appointments and walk through open doors. No man can shut the doors my Father opens for me today. I call into my life those who are called by my side to aid me in my divine destiny. I call alongside myself those who I am assigned to aid in their destiny. I declare anyone who is not part of the destiny the Father has for me exits my life today. I am connected with the right people for the benefit of myself and others.

I declare I walk in and experience the peace of God which surpasses all human understanding. His peace guards my heart and mind. I release the peace of Christ into my home, upon my spouse, children and friends. The peace of God is my umpire today and will not be overruled by any powers or principalities. I declare there is nothing missing, lacking or broken in any area of my life from this day forward. In Jesus' name!

Scriptures for Medication:

Philippians 4:7

And the peace of God, which transcends all understanding, will guard your hearts and your minds in Christ Jesus.

Revelation 3:7

These are the words of him who is holy and true, who holds the key of David. What he opens no one can shut, and what he shuts no one can open.

Day Seven

I decree and declare my steps are ordered by the Lord. He takes me onto a path which leads to pleasant places and green pastures. The blessing of the Lord makes me rich. His blessing is upon me and my household. Wellness goodness favor and prosperity mark my path today. Every area of my life is flourishing and increasing. Therefore, abundance is attracted to me. I am abundant. I am wealthy. I am healthy. I walk in the wisdom of God in every situation.

I declare business opportunities come to me now. Promotion comes to me now. Money comes to me now through various avenues. I declare financial abundance is headed in my direction right now! I expect unexpected income to come me. As I am blessed I am a blessing to others. In Jesus' name!

Scriptures for Medication:

Proverbs 10:22 (KV)
The blessing of the Lord, it maketh rich, and he addeth no sorrow with it.

Psalm 37:23
The Lord makes firm the steps of the one who delights in him

Day Eight

I decree and declare everything which pertains to life and godliness is in me and has been provided for me by my Father. God in me is my rich source of supply. So today, I make a withdrawal from the fountain of grace the Father has placed in me. I declare prosperity flows through me into every area of my life. Financial abundance is attracted to me and comes to me from every direction. Unusual money comes to me. Unusual God ordained ideas come to me. Unusual opportunities come to me today.

The favor of God erupts in every area of my life today and the anointing of multiplication is on everything I set my hands to. Every place I set the sole of my foot today, I declare it is an inheritance for the Kingdom of God. Those who encounter me today come face to face with the blessing of the Lord! In Jesus' name!

Scriptures for Medication:

2 Peter 1:3

According as his divine power hath given unto us all things that pertain unto life and godliness, through the knowledge of him that hath called us to glory and virtue.

Joshua 1:3

I will give you every place where you set your foot, as I promised Moses

Day Nine

I decree and declare I am a king and priest in the earth. I have dominion and power in my region. I am who God says I am and can do what He says I can do. I am the head and not the tail, a lender and not a borrower. I am blessed and highly favored in every area of my life. Wealth and abundance are mine. I see myself as a successful person today. Divine success and prosperity mark my way today. God's abundance flows through me and around me.

I decree and declare I am a demonstration of the abundance of the Kingdom of God. I am wealthy because my Father is wealthy. I am rich because God in me is rich and overflows with abundance. I have abundance for every good work as a giver. I show forth my Father's goodness by freely blessing others. In Jesus' name!

Scriptures for Medication:

Revelation 1:6

And has made us to be a kingdom and priests to serve his God and Father—to him be glory and power forever and ever! Amen.

Deuteronomy 28:12

The Lord will open the heavens, the storehouse of his bounty, to send rain on your land in season and to bless all the work of your hands. You will lend to many nations but will borrow from none.

Day Ten

I command every area of my life to come into perfect alignment with the Word of God. I decree and declare my marriage, children, business, employment, body and finances are flourishing and whole. I declare my finances are operating in line with the Word of God today. This world system is not in control of my money. Only my Father who lives in me is in control of my money. My money is in the Kingdom system and my Father multiplies it every day just like Jesus multiplied the fish and the loaves. I declare I operate in financial excess. I see it and expect it.

I declare as a giver, men are headed in my direction to increase me financially. Everywhere I go I encounter the abundant favor of God. Business comes to me. Opportunities come to me now! My streams of wealth are increasing right now. Wealth, abundance and overflow mark my way today. I believe I receive right now. In Jesus' name!

Scriptures for Medication:

Luke 9:16

Taking the five loaves and the two fish and looking up to heaven, he gave thanks and broke them. Then he gave them to the disciples to distribute to the people.

Luke 6:38

Give, and it will be given to you. A good measure, pressed down, shaken together and running over, will be poured into your lap. For with the measure you use, it will be measured to you."

Day Eleven

I decree and declare the Lord is my Shepherd therefore I shall not and do not want or lack any good thing. Every good and perfect gift has already been provided for me by my Father who lives in and through me. My life is marked by wholeness - perfect peace in every area. He leads me into places of abundance which drip and overflow with His blessing. His goodness and mercy follow me and my household everywhere we go. All who encounter me encounter the love of the Father today.

I decree and declare I have access to an infinite supply of wealth and goods. Because my Father is my rich, endless and infinite supply of all good, every need, want and desire is met beyond my expectation. Every good thing I need to fulfill my purpose and plan has been richly provided for me. I declare I have great wealth and honor. In Jesus' name!

Scriptures for Medication

James 1:17

Every good and perfect gift is from above, coming down from the Father of the heavenly lights, who does not change like shifting shadows.

Psalm 23

The Lord is my shepherd, I lack nothing.

Day Twelve

I decree and declare I am the prosperous, healthy child of I AM. My finances operate according to God's divine order. I declare God's wisdom is at work in and through me, to guide me in every financial decision. I set my heart and mind on things above today. I do not mediate on lack, want or need. Today my mind is set on my Father's plans and purposes for my life. Therefore my provision is always amply supplied. I decree and declare the righteous are never forsaken and my seed will never beg for bread.

My mind is clear today to receive God ideas, inventions, business opportunities, and solutions. My household is surrounded by my Father's divine substance and it manifests for us richly and openly in every area of our lives. My family boldly walks in the blessing of the Lord for all to see. In Jesus' name!

Scriptures for Medication

Joshua 1:8

Keep this Book of the Law always on your lips; meditate
on it day and night, so that you may be careful to do
everything written in it. Then you will be
prosperous and successful.

Psalm 37:25

I was young and now I am old, yet I have never seen
the righteous forsaken
or their children begging bread.

Day Thirteen

I decree and declare I am walking in total restoration in every area of my life. Everything the enemy has stolen from me is restored seven-fold right now! God is for me and no one can be against me. Today I receive and accept by faith, my inheritance, both spiritual and natural. I expect abundance to overtake me today. I expect the work of my hands to manifest wealth, abundance and overflow today. I declare I am a walking demonstration of the infinite love, power and abundance of my Father.

I declare my Father has already cleared the way for me to experience the blessing. It's my divine birthright to walk in and manifest my Father's rich glory in my finances, marriage and with my children. By faith I come into agreement with Him and accept my divine right to experience His rich blessing. I am a blessing waiting to happen for someone today, in Jesus' name!

Scriptures for Medication

Proverbs 6:31

Yet if he is caught, he must pay sevenfold, though it costs him all the wealth of his house.

Isaiah 54:2 (KJV)

Enlarge the place of your tent, stretch your tent curtains wide, do not hold back; lengthen your cords, strengthen your stakes.

Day Fourteen

I decree and declare I look away from the downward appearance of lack, shortage and limitation and look upward to the unlimited, infinite source of God in me. I set my heart and mind on Jesus the author and finisher of my faith. I do not participate in unemployment, lack or recession. My supply is not limited in any way by the world's economic condition. The abundant presence of my Father in me causes me to attract wealth, favor and increase everywhere I go today.

I decree and declare I am about the Father's business, multiplying, creating and speaking His word to create my own prosperous world today. I release His prosperous words over my family, employment and business. I declare every area of my life is subject to Divine increase and multiplication for the Kingdom of God. I see my good as it comes forth for me and my household right now. Every area of my life resembles the God kind of life, in Jesus' name!

Scriptures for Medication

John 10:10

"I have come that they may have life, and have it to the full."

Genesis 1:28

God blessed them and said to them, "Be fruitful and increase in number; fill the earth and subdue it. Rule over the fish in the sea and the birds in the sky and over every living creature that moves on the ground."

Day Fifteen

I decree and declare I do not depend on any person or condition as the source of my supply. My Heavenly Father is my one and only Source of supply. He has ALREADY blessed me with all manner of blessing in the realm of the spirit which is the originating place of all natural things. I declare the abundance of God flows from within me producing such an abundant outpouring that my cup runs over today. A table of blessing has been prepared for me in the presence of my enemies as proof of my Father's provision for His children.

I decree and declare I am planted like a tree by the living water and receive a constant and superabundant flow of health, prosperity, encouragement, financial abundance and peace. All doors of God's bounty are open for me today. Nothing can intercept, hinder, or derail the good my Father has coming my way. As my cup runs over, I serve and bless others. In Jesus name!

Scriptures for Medication

Psalm 23:5

You prepare a table before me in the presence of my enemies. You anoint my head with oil; my cup overflows.

Ephesians 1:3

Praise be to the God and Father of our Lord Jesus Christ, who has blessed us in the heavenly realms with every spiritual blessing in Christ.

Day Sixteen

I decree and declare I see myself blessed in every way. I see my children blessed and walking in the favor of God. I see my marriage prospering. I see myself wealthy, walking in the abundant overflow of my loving Heavenly Father. This same favor is at work in my business and at my place of employment. I see myself receiving promotion, contracts, gifts in the mail and divine opportunities today.

Now, I speak into existence that which I see inwardly, just as my Heavenly Father did. I declare, let there be, and amen to the provision the Father has put in place for me. Every creative word I release into the atmosphere must come forth in my Father's perfect timing. I have confident expectation my Father will never leave or forsake me. He lives in me and walks along side me. I am never without or lacking. I always operate from a position of financial surplus. I declare I receive right now to the full and overflowing. I am blessed to be a blessing until all nations of the earth are blessed. In Jesus' name!

Scriptures for Medication

Genesis 1:3-4

And God said, "Let there be light," and there was light.
God saw that the light was good…

Job 22:28 (KJV)

Thou shalt also decree a thing, and it shall be established
unto thee: and the light shall shine upon thy ways.

Day Seventeen

I decree and declare I am successful and prosperous in all things. I only desire the good the Father has for me. I do not compete with others but help to complete their divine assignment. There is enough of my Father's abundance for His children. I refuse to accept any limiting circumstances which are contrary to the prosperous truths of my Father's Word. Whatever situations I encounter today I declare I receive divine instruction and solutions to create a prosperous outcome.

I decree and declare I am a money master. I handle my finances skillfully for my Father. Money is not my master. I do not run after money because it is attracted to me. Men are favorably disposed to bless me because I am a giver. My money is on divine assignment to be fruitful and to multiply for my household and the Kingdom of God. I listen to the voice of my Father as He guides me to bless others. God's almighty power goes before me, making easy, successful and delightful my way. In Jesus' name!

Scriptures for Medication

Matthew 6:24

No man can serve two masters: for either he will hate the one, and love the other; or else he will hold to the one, and despise the other. Ye cannot serve God and mammon.

John 5:19

"Very truly I tell you, the Son can do nothing by himself; he can do only what he sees his Father doing, because whatever the Father does the Son also does.

Day Eighteen

I decree and declare I am now shown new ways of living and new methods of working today. I am not confined to the ways and methods of the past or the ways and methods of men. My work is fruitful and bountifully and rewarded richly by my Heavenly Father. I declare I will not put up with or tolerate any adverse financial circumstances which last more than a night. I refuse to accept anything contrary to my Father's Word. I am God's child and will not accept anything but His complete goodness for me.

I decree and declare I am a manifestor of covenant wealth today. Divine doors open up for me and I boldly step through them. I do not walking blindly, but I walk by faith as I see through the lenses of the Word of God. God ideas come to me today and I act upon them. I freely and willingly bless those who encounter me today. In Jesus' name!

Scriptures for Medication

Psalm 37:23

**The Lord makes firm the steps of the one
who delights in him**

2 Corinthians 5:7

For we live by faith, not by sight.

Day Nineteen

I invite the loving action of my Heavenly Father into my life today. Because God is with me and lives in me, I expect the best and attract the best in every situation. Nothing can keep my Father's good from flowing into my life today. I tap into my Father's infinite supply of health, wealth, wisdom and prosperity, because this is my inheritance as a child of God.

I decree and declare all financial doors are open for me today. All financial channels are free. My Father's endless supply comes to men now. It can't be intercepted or opposed by outside forces. Money and various opportunities are drawn to me today. My money is making money, making money. Compound Interest is no longer at work against me but for me. Nothing but the best comes to me in every area of my life. In Jesus' name!

Scriptures for Medication

Malachi 3:11 (KJV)

And I will rebuke the devourer for your sakes, and he shall not destroy the fruits of your ground; neither shall your vine cast her fruit before the time in the field, saith the LORD of hosts.

3 John 1:2

Beloved, I wish above all things that thou mayest prosper and be in health, even as thy soul prospereth.

Day Twenty

I decree and declare God's super abounding grace rests upon me and my household in every area of our lives. Our bodies are subject to and submissive to God's grace. Our relationships are governed by His grace. My children are directed by God's grace. My finances are increasing and multiplying because of His grace.

I decree and declare the anointing of multiplication is on my money. My investments are multiplying and my interest compounds daily. My streams of income increase daily. My money flows like streams of rushing water. It's picking up money as it is circulated in the economy and comes back to me pressed down, shaken together and running over. Because I freely give, men continually move in my direction to bless me abundantly. I am filled to capacity and am in the position of overflow to be a blessing to others. In Jesus' name!

Scriptures for Medication

2 Peter 2: 1-4 (KJV)

Grace and peace be multiplied unto you through the knowledge of God, and of Jesus our Lord, According as his divine power hath given unto us all things that pertain unto life and godliness, through the knowledge of him that hath called us to glory and virtue Whereby are given unto us exceeding great and precious promises: that by these ye might be partakers of the divine nature, having escaped the corruption that is in the world through lust.

Day Twenty-One

I decree and declare I am a vessel my Father works through today. I do not withhold His good from others. I am obedient to His purpose and desire to use me to bless others. I willingly use my resources as directed by God, to be a blessing to others. I declare all He has given me is at his disposal. I am not captured or enslaved by things, money or any other vice. I am not a slave to anything or anyone except Christ Jesus.

I decree and declare as a vessel of the Most High God, my financial resources flow to me and through me. I am overtaken by my Father's abundance. His good comes to me from every possible direction. I do not resist His goodness. I openly receive and accept all the good He is sending my way today. I declare my good comes back to me multiplied in an unending cycle of increase and abundance so I may continually be a blessing to others. In Jesus' name!

Scriptures for Medication

2 Corinthians 9:10-11 (KJV)

Now he that ministereth seed to the sower both minister bread for your food, and multiply your seed sown, and increase the fruits of your righteousness. Being enriched in every thing to all bountifulness, which causeth through us thanksgiving to God.

Genesis 12:2

I will make you into a great nation, and I will bless you; I will make your name great, and you will be a blessing.

Day Twenty-Two

I decree and declare I am experiencing a prosperity demonstration in every area of my life today! I am keenly aware of the goodness of God at work in and through my life. I declare I am experiencing a divine demonstration of abundant overflow as I follow the voice of the Holy Spirit today. I am open and receptive to His divine guidance and provision. I expect nothing but God's best in all that I do today.

I decree and declare I am the recipient of unlimited increase in my mind, health and finances today. Right here and right now I open myself to the goodness of the God of love. He has given me all the riches of life to enjoy. I am open to receive the wealth that flows all around me. I see myself today as my Father sees me, having all of the abundance and wealth that is mine. Because I am financially blessed, I am able to respond to every good cause. I receive today by faith. In Jesus' name!

Scriptures for Medication

Hebrews 1:36
You need to persevere so that when you have done the will of God, you will receive what he has promised.

Galatians 3:29
If you belong to Christ, then you are Abraham's seed, and heirs according to the promise.

Day Twenty-Three

I decree and declare today to be a special day, a perfect day, because God in me is leading and guiding me along a straight path. His ways are perfect. His Word is perfect. I yield myself, my family, business, children, job and finances to the infinite wisdom of the great I AM. He is whatever I need Him to be in my life today. Every situation, every need and desire has already been settled in heaven by His infallible Word. Therefore, I walk in peace today.

I decree and declare I have no financial limits or boundaries. I am like the streams of the Negev, flowing freely financially and I am experiencing financial restoration today. I declare I have been redeemed from the curse of lack, debt and poverty. The blessing of my forefather Abraham rests upon me and my household. I am very rich today like my father Abraham. I declare I have employees, multiple streams of income, stocks, bonds and a lucrative investment portfolio. In Jesus' name!

Scriptures for Medication

Psalm 126:4

Restore our fortunes, Lord, like streams in the Negev.

Exodus 3:14

God said to Moses, "I am who I am. This is what you are to say to the Israelites: 'I am has sent me to you.'"

Day Twenty-Four

I decree and declare my Father wants nothing but the best for me. He is not withholding anything from me. He gave His only Son for me and has freely given me, in Him, all things to enjoy. Everything God has given to Jesus He has also been willed to me. Therefore I declare I live a life of plenty in every area.

I decree and declare my financial resources flow to me from various regions of this nation. I am not limited by a job, paycheck or people. I am not limited by my geographical area, race or position. I do not envy the financial manifestation of others, but celebrate and bless them. Nothing can keep me from the abundant blessing my Father has decreed over my life. I speak these rich, life giving words to my finances today: I command my money to come to me now. I declare my money is headed in my direction right now. As I am enriched I am a blessing to others. In Jesus' name!

Scriptures for Medication

2 Corinthians 8:9

For you know the grace of our Lord Jesus Christ, that though he was rich, yet for your sake he became poor, so that you through his poverty might become rich.

Romans 8:32

He who did not spare his own Son, but gave him up for us all—how will he not also, along with him, graciously give us all things?

Day Twenty-Five

I decree and declare I have dominion and power over the enemy and nothing shall by any means hurt me. As an ambassador for Christ, I am on Kingdom assignment today to show forth my Father's glory and goodness. Everything I need is attracted in my life. I have no needs, desires or wants because my Father has amply provided for me and my household. I walk in the lavish blessing and abundant favor of my Father.

I declare today, I expect and experience nothing but the Father's best. I seek first the Kingdom of God – His righteousness and His way of doing and being right today. As a result, all the material things needed for my assignment and enjoyment are added to my life. The blessing of the Lord has made me rich and I do not toil to receive or experience it. In Jesus' name!

Scriptures for Medication

Matthew 6:33
But seek first his kingdom and his righteousness, and all these things will be given to you as well.

Proverbs 10:22
The blessing of the Lord brings wealth,
without painful toil for it.

Day Twenty-Six

I decree and declare I am now experiencing divine health and abundant prosperity in every area of my life. God's divine favor is released over every endeavor and over my sphere of influence. I declare ministering angels are at work on my behalf today to carry out the Word God has spoken over me. Men who can aid me in my God-given assignment are moving in my direction to impart wisdom and direction. I willingly embrace their divine assignment to aid me.

I decree and declare I come into my inheritance today. I embrace the life and life more abundantly my Father has prepared for me. This day I decide to accept and walk in my financial prosperity. My money is increasing daily. I am now living a delightful, interesting and satisfying life which is pleasing and acceptable to God. Because I have embraced my financial inheritance I am now able to help others live a God-kind of life also. In Jesus' name!

Scriptures for Medication

Hebrews 1:14

Are not all angels ministering spirits sent to serve those
who will inherit salvation?

Ephesians 5:10-11

And find out what pleases the Lord. Have nothing to do
with the fruitless deeds of darkness, but rather expose them.

Day Twenty-Seven

I decree and declare I am a magnet for wealth, good health abundance, favor and money because the infinite, abundant God lives in me. God who lives in me is an attractor of good things; therefore no good thing can be withheld from me. Everything needed for the plan the Father has prepared for me is already in place. As I allow my steps to be ordered, my provision is sure. As I walk in my Father's way, a prosperous path is opened up before me.

I decree and declare I have been created in the image and likeness of my Father with the ability to speak things into existence and create my world. Therefore I boldly declare life, health and strength in my body, marriage, in the lives of my children and those whom I will encounter today. I lay hold of the nations as my inheritance and the uttermost parts of the earth as my possession. I declare I take this as a possession for the Kingdom of God. In Jesus' name!

Scriptures for Medication

Psalm 84:11

For the LORD God is a sun and shield; the LORD bestows favor and honor; no good thing does he withhold from those whose walk is blameless.

Psalm 2:8 (KJV)

Ask me, and I will make the nations your inheritance, the ends of the earth your possession.

Day Twenty-Eight

I decree and declare the super abounding multifaceted (many sided) grace of God is at work in every area of my life today. I am flowing in the abundant blessing God has planned and declared over my household. I come into agreement with His prosperous plans for my life today by speaking His Word only. I only speak what the Father has spoken over me and avoid all negative conversation contrary to His Word. I declare I use my tongue as the pen of a ready writer and I declare prosperous outcomes in my life today.

I declare my finances prosper and increase today. I attract wealth, unexpected income, gifts in the mail, and unusual favor today. I declare I am breaking out abundantly on every side in everything I set out to do. I can't be stopped, detained or hindered today because it's my Father's will for me to prosper in every area. My God in me and who is with me, goes before me and levels every mountain and obstacle in my way. As I am blessed I look to be a blessing to others. In Jesus' name!

Scriptures for Medication

Psalm 45:1

My heart is stirred by a noble theme as I recite my verses
for the king; my tongue is the pen of a skillful writer.

Isaiah 45:1-3

I will go before you and will level the mountains; I will
break down gates of bronze and cut through bars of iron. I
will give you hidden treasures,
riches stored in secret places, so that you may know that
I am the Lord,
the God of Israel, who summons you by name.

Day Twenty-Nine

I decree and declare I give my Father great pleasure today because I prosper in all things. I speak and see myself abundantly supplied for every good work and purpose of God. I speak and see my children living according to the Word of God. I speak the Word of God over my spouse and I see him/her flourishing in their divine destiny. I see them fulfilling their kingdom assignment on this earth. I release the blessing of the Lord upon those I encounter today even if their behavior or lifestyle is contrary to the Word of God. As I release the living Word of God over them, their life will be transformed.

I speak and see financial increase today. I speak and see my money making money and increasing. I decree and declare I own lands and houses, commercial and income properties. Every investment I am involved in can't help but multiply and every contract comes to completion as expected. I declare I am loaded up with the benefits of the God of my salvation. As a result, my abundance flows over into the lives of others. In Jesus' name!

Scriptures for Medication

Psalm 35:27

May those who delight in my vindication shout for joy and gladness; may they always say, "The LORD be exalted, who delights in the well-being of his servant."

Romans 12:14

Bless those who persecute you; bless and do not curse.

Day Thirty

I decree and declare I accept the highest and best in life. I make a conscious decision to accept the healing Jesus has already provided for me. I accept His blood sacrifice which covered every area of my life. I choose to accept health, success and happiness. My mouth is satisfied with good things. Today I rearrange, transform and rebuild anything which does not come into direct agreement and alignment with the Word of God, by declaring His Word only. I will not permit others to define my life. Nor will I conform to a not enough or just enough mentality.

I decree and declare I release all opposition to wealth. Wealth is my birth-right, my natural state of being and doing. I now choose lavish abundance for myself and for those around me. I accept and embrace wealth, money and abundance with open arms. I declare I have been brought out of poverty, lack and insufficiency into my wealthy place. Today I am established in a place of abundance and increase. In Jesus' name!

Scriptures for Medication

Romans 12:2

Do not conform to the pattern of this world,
but be transformed by the renewing of your mind.

Psalm 66:12

You let people ride over our heads; we went through fire
and water, but you brought us to a place of abundance.

Day Thirty-One

I decree and declare that my thoughts lend themselves only to what is plenteous. I mediate on whatsoever is good, true, noble right, pure, lovely, and admirable. If anything is excellent or praiseworthy this is what I choose to think about today. As I meditate on what is good, it manifests itself all around me. I see abundance all around me. I see a life of happiness and wholeness making its way from the inside to the outside. I declare I am creating the life of my dreams through my prosperous thoughts and words.

I decree and declare wealth flows into my hands freely. An abundance of money comes to me easily and effortlessly. In all instances, I see my income continually increasing. All of my financial needs, desires, and goals are met beyond anything I can imagine. I have plenty and am satisfied because the Lord has dealt bountifully with me. I declare I can be, do and have everything the Father has for me. I am an excellent giver and receiver of money and gifts, therefore I declare myself wealthy in Jesus' name!

Philippians 4:8

Finally, brothers and sisters, whatever is true, whatever is noble, whatever is right, whatever is pure, whatever is lovely, whatever is admirable—if anything is excellent or praiseworthy—think about such things

Psalm 13:6 (KJV)
I will sing unto the LORD, because he hath dealt bountifully with me.

About the Author

Sonya L Thompson was born in Paterson, New Jersey. She is an ordained minister, best-selling author, successful entrepreneur and key note speaker. Sonya holds a B.S. in the field of Business Administration and is a Servant Leader at Hope International Church in Groveland Florida. She has appeared on "With God You Will Succeed," with renowned author and speaker, Dr. Tom Leding. She has also been a special guest on several Christian radio stations.

Sonya has been serving the Lord for 21 years and has a passion to share the "Living Word", which has transformed her life, with the body of Christ. Her desire is to see the body of Christ become manifestors of the Kingdom of God, in order to draw the unsaved to the Father. Her calling is to "Train, Educate and Advise through the Gospel with Simplicity and Purity."

Other Books By Sonya L. Thompson

Break Out of Poverty Into Financial Abundance

Business By The Bible

Seeds Of Prosperity Book & CD

Glory Walkers Revealed

To Order visit:

www.oilandtheglory.com

Also available on Amazon

Notes

_____

_____

_____

_____

_____

_____

_____

_____

_____

_____

_____

_____

_____

_____

_____

_____

_____

_____

_____

Notes

Notes

Notes

Notes

Notes

Notes

Made in the USA
Middletown, DE
14 April 2016